WHALES!
STRANGE AND WONDERFUL

Laurence Pringle

Illustrated by **Meryl Henderson**

BOYDS MILLS PRESS
HONESDALE, PENNSYLVANIA

Dedicated with deep gratitude to all who helped and inspired me on an amazing journey that now leads to publication of this, my one hundredth book. Far too numerous to mention by name, they include my parents, children, and wife, Susan, friends, teachers, mentors, librarians, scientists, editors, book designers, artists, and fellow writers.

—LP

To my sister Beth and her husband, Tom, who have dedicated their lives to preserving America's wild places and her precious wild animals

—MH

The author wishes to thank Dr. James Darling, West Coast Whale Research Foundation, and Dr. Edward O. Keith, Oceanographic Center, Nova Southeastern University, for their gracious assistance to both author and artist.

Boyds Mills Press, Inc.
815 Church Street
Honesdale, Pennsylvania 18431
Printed in China
boydsmillspress.com

Publisher Cataloging-in-Publication Data (U.S)

Pringle, Laurence.
  Whales! strange and wonderful / by Laurence Pringle ; illustrated by Meryl Henderson.—1st ed.
[32] p. : col. Ill. ; cm.
Summary: Discusses species, physiognomy, and behavior of whales.
ISBN: 978-1-56397-439-7 (hc) • ISBN: 978-1-59078-917-9 (pb)
1. Whales—Juvenile literature. (1. Whales.) I. Henderson, Meryl. II. Title.
599.53/ 6 21 AC CIP 2003
2002105798

First Boyds Mills Press paperback edition, 2012
The text of this book is set in Clearface.

10 9 8 7 6 5 4 3 2 1

Bowhead whale—
up to 60 feet long

If you were a giant whale, you could open your mouth wide enough to hold an elephant. You could dive deep in the ocean and hold your breath for more than an hour.

Blowhole

Top view of blowholes

Flipper

Then you would swim to the surface and take a deep breath. Although whales live in water, they are not fish. They are mammals, like you, and cannot breathe underwater.

When a whale rises to the surface to breathe, it blows waste air from its lungs out through one or two special holes on top of its head called blowholes, which are like the nostrils of your nose. *Whoosh!* A powerful burst of water vapor sprays into the air. Then the whale breathes in fresh air through its blowholes.

Dorsal fin

Tail

Flukes

Fin whale—
up to 72 feet long

5

Humpback whale—
up to 50 feet long

Killer whale—
up to 32 feet long

Long-finned pilot whale—
up to 20 feet long

Blue whale—
up to 100 feet long

About eighty species, or kinds, of whales swim in Earth's oceans. Scientists call them cetaceans (see-TAY-shuns), from a Latin word for whale. Cetaceans include whales, dolphins, and porpoises. They come in many sizes and shapes. Some have dorsal, or back, fins. Others do not.

Some dolphins and porpoises measure less than six feet long—about as long as an adult person is tall. Other cetaceans are enormous. The water supports their huge bodies so they can grow bigger than any animals that live on land.

Baird's beaked whale—
up to 42 feet long

Franciscana—
up to 6 feet long

Dall's porpoise—
up to 7 feet long

Sperm whale—
up to 60 feet long

Beluga—
up to 17 feet long

Most cetaceans have teeth for catching fish, squid, and other prey animals. These toothed whales have just one blowhole. Toothed whales, which include dolphins and porpoises, are very sociable. They usually travel and hunt together in groups.

The toothed whales called belugas often live in cold Arctic waters. Their white skin may help them hide from the killer whales and polar bears that hunt them in the jumbled sea ice of the Arctic. The name *beluga* comes from a Russian word for white.

Juvenile

Beluga—
up to 16 feet long

Juvenile

Female

Male

Narwhal—
up to 16 feet long

Narwhals also live in the Arctic. They have just two big teeth in their upper jaws. As a male narwhal becomes an adult, its right tooth stops growing, but its left tooth does not. It pushes through the narwhal's upper lip, then keeps growing—longer and longer, until it forms a tusk that may measure as long as nine feet.

Orcas are called killer whales, but they are actually the biggest of all dolphins. A newborn orca is longer than a man is tall, and an adult male is nearly as long as a big school bus.

Killer whales have forty or more big, sharp teeth. They usually hunt in a group, like a pack of wolves, and sometimes attack dolphins and small whales. Orcas also eat penguins, sea lions, squid, and fish. They are fierce killers, but are usually playful and gentle with people, and can be easily trained to perform in aquarium shows.

Killer whales hunting sea lions

Sperm whales are giants—the biggest of all toothed whales. The females are about the length of a big school bus. The males are double that size, and may weigh up to sixty tons. Sperm whales have short, stubby flippers but are huge in many other ways. Their massive heads alone make up a third of their length. They have the largest brain (weighing 20 pounds) and the thickest skin (14 inches) of any animal on Earth. They also have a huge appetite, eating hundreds of pounds of octopus and squid each day.

Sperm whales may stay underwater for more than an hour and hunt a mile or more beneath the surface. They sometimes catch giant squid in the ocean's dark depths.

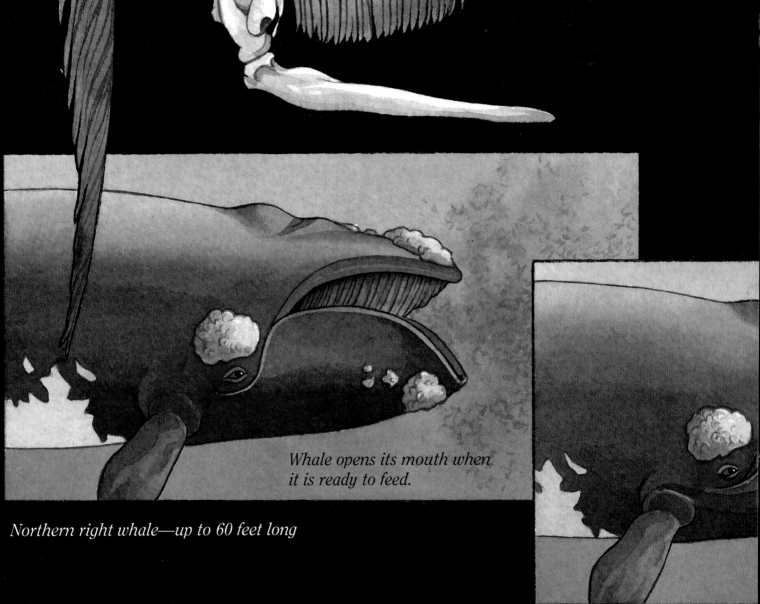

Whale opens its mouth when it is ready to feed.

Northern right whale—up to 60 feet long

Nine species of whales have no teeth, yet they eat well, and some grow to be the biggest whales of all. They are called baleen (bay-LEEN) whales. Baleen is sometimes called whalebone, but it is not bone. It is keratin, the same strong but flexible material that your fingernails are made of. Many plates of baleen hang from a whale's upper jaws. The baleen plates look like giant curtains, lined up like the pages of a book.

A baleen whale eats by taking a mouthful of water. Its giant tongue and cheek muscles then force the water through the baleen and out the sides of its mouth. The fringed edges of the baleen act like a filter or sieve. Small fish and other little animals in the water are trapped by the baleen, then swallowed.

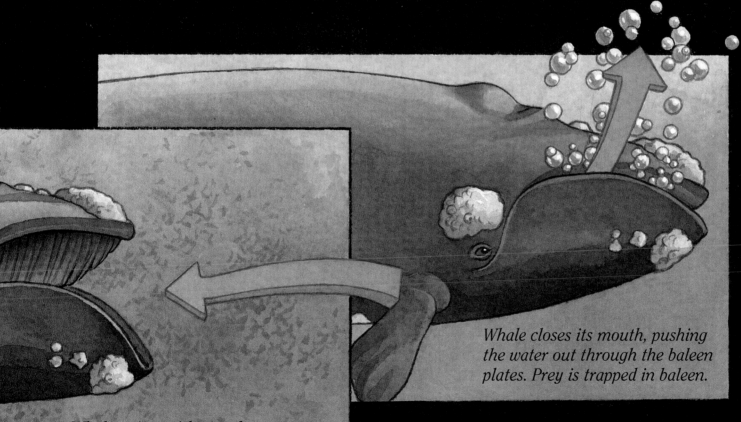

Whale closes its mouth, pushing the water out through the baleen plates. Prey is trapped in baleen.

Whale swims with mouth open, taking in water mixed with prey.

In the far north, and in the far south, near Antarctica, baleen whales catch many small animals called copepods and krill. Vast swarms of these animals feed near the surface in the summertime. Right whales swim with their heads partway out of the water and their mouths open. They trap thousands of tiny animals in each mouthful of water.

One or more humpback whales may swim in a circle beneath a swarm of krill or a school of small fish. They let air out of their blowholes. Streams of air bubbles rise, causing the krill or fish to crowd together in the center of the circle. Then the whales lunge upward with their mouths open to engulf their prey.

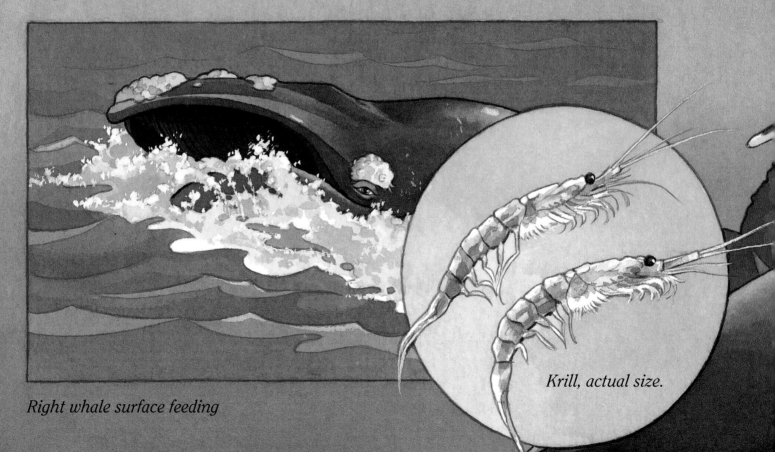

Right whale surface feeding

Krill, actual size.

Humpback whales
making bubble net

The blue whale is the largest of all baleen whales. It can grow to be 100 feet long and weigh 160 tons. That makes it heavier than thirty elephants. Its tongue alone weighs as much as an elephant! For many years the blue whale was called the biggest animal that ever lived, but now scientists believe that some dinosaurs grew to be as long or longer.

The giant blue whale has a giant appetite. It often swallows a hundred pounds of krill in one gulp. It may eat four tons of krill in one day.

Risso's dolphin—
up to 12 feet long

Blue whale —
up to 100 feet long

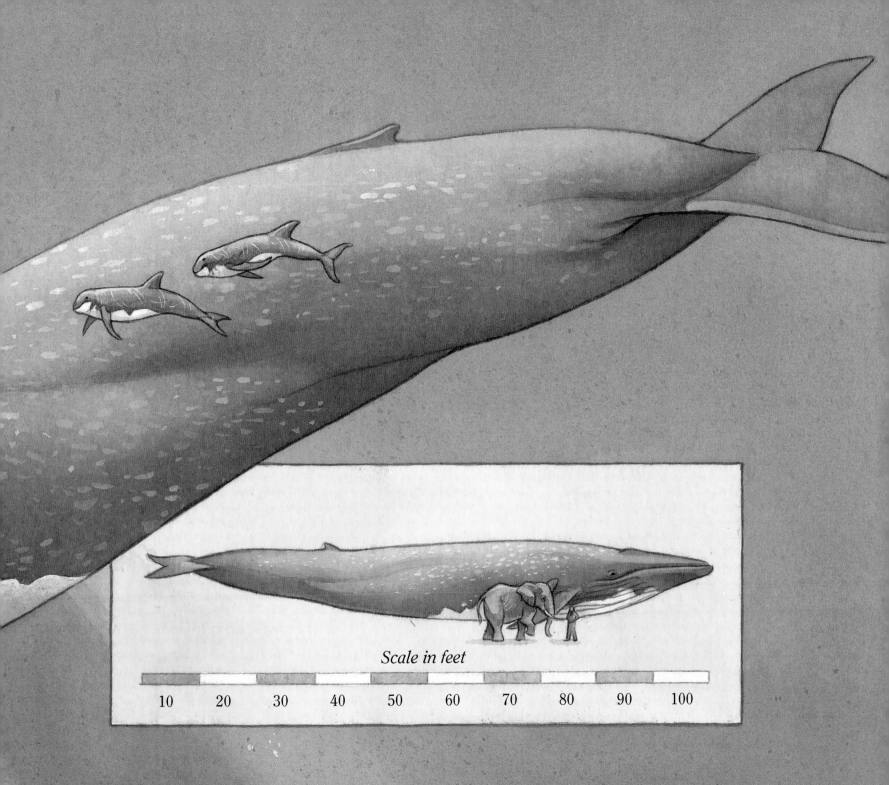

Scale in feet

10   20   30   40   50   60   70   80   90   100

*A dolphin listens to echoes
to find a squid.*

The biggest whale of all also has the loudest voice. Some people who have heard the grunt of a blue whale say it is louder than the roar of a jet engine. All cetaceans have the ability to hear and to make sounds. Underwater, sound travels much farther and five times faster than it does in air. Near or far, members of a group of whales can call to one another.

The sounds of some whales also help them find their way underwater and to locate food. Dolphins and other toothed whales listen to the echoes of their calls. From the echoes they can learn what lies ahead—perhaps a school of fish or a dangerous shark.

In the Arctic, beluga whales are able to use the echoes of their sounds to find open breathing spaces in the ice. Belugas bray, buzz, click, squawk, warble, yelp, and trill. Sailors call belugas "sea canaries" because of their birdlike whistles.

Bowhead whales can imitate the calls of other whales. During the mating season of humpback whales, the male humpbacks bellow, creak, moan, and whistle. Their complex songs may be thirty minutes long, and change each year. Some people think the humpback has the most beautiful of all animal songs.

Atlantic spotted dolphin—
up to 8 feet long

Humpback whales

22

Huge whales sometimes lunge out of the water, then fall back with a great splash. This is called breaching. It often happens during mating season, when males try to impress females, but both males and females breach at other times, too.

When a baby whale (called a calf) is born, it emerges tail first from its mother's body. Its mother, and sometimes other female whales, push the calf up to the surface. There it takes its first breath. The mother may swim beneath her calf, supporting it until it can swim well by itself.

A whale calf eats "fast food." It closes its blowhole and dives down to its mother's belly for its first meal. When the calf finds a nipple, the mother squirts plenty of rich milk into its mouth. Soon the calf must swim up for air. It may have as many as forty quick meals a day.

Mother whales keep their calves close and try to protect them from sharks and other enemies. Like other young animals, including human children, whale calves are curious and playful.

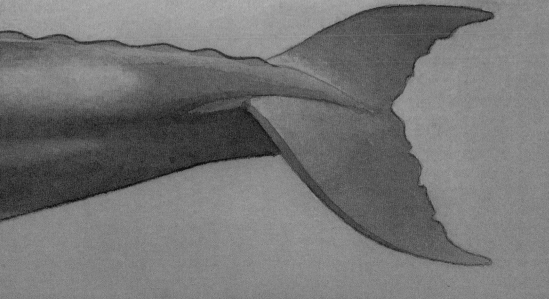

Migration route of gray whales:
• Northward between February and June
• Southward between November and January

Most baleen whale calves are born in the winter, in warm waters near Earth's equator, or middle. In the spring, groups of whales swim toward colder waters near the poles. They swim slowly so the calves can keep up.

The whales feast on plentiful krill and other prey. They gain weight and store fat that gives them energy for the long autumn southward journey. In their back-and-forth travels, called migration, whales may swim thousands of miles. Gray whales migrate between the Arctic Ocean and the western coast of Mexico, a round-trip distance of up to 12,000 miles. They often swim close to shore.

As whales swim, they are protected from cold by blubber, a thick layer of fat beneath their skin. Blubber was once highly valued by people. They killed whales for blubber and boiled it to make oil. Whale oil was used to make candles, soap, paint, lipstick, and fuel for oil lamps that lit homes and city streets. Whale baleen was used in making brushes, corsets, buggy whips, and umbrellas.

Killing a whale was once a great challenge. Men on sailing ships searched the seas for whales. When one was seen, rowboats were launched. The whalers tried to row close enough to a whale so a man could hurl a sharp harpoon into its body.

Two similar kinds of baleen whales were favorite targets of whaling ships. One species lived in the northern half of Earth, the other in the southern half. Both whales swam slowly. Their plentiful blubber helped keep them afloat after being killed. They became known as the right whales to hunt, and today are still called right whales.

Whalers hunting a right whale

Factory ship hauling in blue whales

In the 1800s and especially in the 1900s, people developed new ways of finding and killing whales. In the second half of the twentieth century, airplanes or helicopters spotted whales from above. Fast powerboats chased and killed them with explosive harpoons. Dead whales were hauled aboard giant ships on which meat, blubber, and other parts of many whales could be processed and preserved.

The numbers of Earth's largest whales dropped sharply. More than 200,000 blue whales swam the oceans in 1900. By 1967, only about 6,000 were left. As blue whales became scarce, whaling ships began to hunt other large whales until scientists warned that not only blue whales, but also right, bowhead, and humpback whales were in danger of extinction.

Imagine Earth without whales! This is unthinkable to scientists who know them well and to many other people who care about these intelligent, fascinating mammals. They tried to persuade countries to stop killing whales. Gradually, one nation after another gave up commercial whaling. Most whale hunting ended in 1983.

Whales reproduce slowly, but their numbers have begun to rise. People hope that we will always be able to hear whales singing and see these gentle giants of the seas.

WHALE FINDER

Gray whale—
up to 46 feet

More about Whales and Their Conservation

There is reason to hope that numbers of Earth's biggest whales will recover. As whale populations grow, the nations of the world will have to decide whether, or how much, whale hunting is allowed.

There are now substitutes for whale oil, baleen, and other materials that whales once provided, but some whales are still hunted for meat. Both Norway and Japan kill hundreds of minke whales each year, while ignoring requests to stop from the other nations that make up the International Whaling Commission. Minke whales are an abundant baleen species. In the year 2000, Japan also began killing whales of two other species, Bryde's and sperm whales. All of Japan's whale hunts are done in the name of research. However, the whale meat is sold in stores and restaurants, and conservation groups claim that Japan's "research" is just another name for commercial whaling.

Other species of cetaceans face different threats. For example, each year many thousands of dolphins die when they become entangled in fishing nets. Both large and small whales can also be harmed by water pollution. Human-made sounds in the water may also harm whales. Loud sounds made by ships may cause whales to become stranded in shallow water. Sometimes a whole group of fifty dolphins or other cetaceans becomes stranded on a beach. Many or all of them die. Historical records show that whale strandings occurred long before humans began using engines in the sea. However, certain stranding incidents have been linked to noise from passing ships.

Each year several million people from more than sixty countries go on whale-watching trips. The sighting of one whale may attract numerous boats. Tour boat operators are urged to stay at least a hundred yards away from whales and to take other steps to avoid harm to their hearing. When these rules are followed, whales can go about their normal lives while people experience the thrill of seeing whales in the wild.

For more information about whales and whale conservation efforts, contact:

- American Cetacean Society, PO Box 1391, San Pedro, CA 90733, acsonline.org*
- Cetacean Society International, PO Box 953, Georgetown, CT 06829, csiwhalesalive.org
- Cousteau Society, 732 Eden Way North, Suite E, #707, Chesapeake, VA 23320, cousteau.org
- Greenpeace USA, 702 H Street NW, Suite 300, Washington, DC 20001, greenpeace.org
- The International Marine Mammal Project, 2150 Allston Way, Suite 460, Berkeley, CA 94704, earthisland.org/immp
- Sea Shepherd Conservation Society, PO Box 2616, Friday Harbor, WA 98250, seashepherd.org

Websites active at time of publication

Did you know that about eighty species of whales swim in Earth's oceans?
A giant whale can open its mouth wide enough to hold an elephant, and
can hold its breath for more than an hour. Some whales have no teeth.
Others have a tusk. These and many other *strange* and *wonderful* facts will
introduce you to the world of this fascinating mammal.

Praise for *Whales! Strange and Wonderful*

"Pringle does a bang up job. . . . It's as wonderful as the whales."
—*Kirkus Reviews*

"A narrative linked with context-rich art shows whales' magnificence in their
natural habitats and encourages conservation. . . . Recommended."
—*Horn Book Guide*

"Well, here is another winner from Laurence Pringle! . . . Highly recommended."
—*Library Media Connection*

Cover illustration copyright © 2011 by Meryl Henderson

$9.95

ISBN 978-1-59078-917-9

50995

9 781590 789179

BOYDS MILLS PRESS
815 Church Street
Honesdale, Pennsylvania 18431
Printed in China
boydsmillspress.com